Colorful Swearing Dreams

Swear Word Coloring Book for Adults

IS YOUR STRESS LEVEL HIGH?
DO YOU WANT TO SWEAR OUT LOUD
TO LEVEL IT DOWN?
THIS BOOK WILL KICK YOUR STRESS AWAY!

Multiple studies revealed that coloring mandalas, geometric patterns & other shapes helps reduce stress and anxiety for adults.

This swear word coloring book will allow you to enter in a relaxed state by focusing in what you are doing and blocking out the nonstop thinking or other distractions. Those swear word designs will make you laugh and relieve your stress by expelling your negative thoughts.

This book contains 20 pages of beautiful & intricate designs mixing up with funny swear words that will connect with you.
Each page is single-sided for getting the best coloring experience.

TIME TO COLOR THE STRESS AWAY!

Colorful Swearing Dreams

Swear Word Coloring Book for Adults

Coloring Test Page

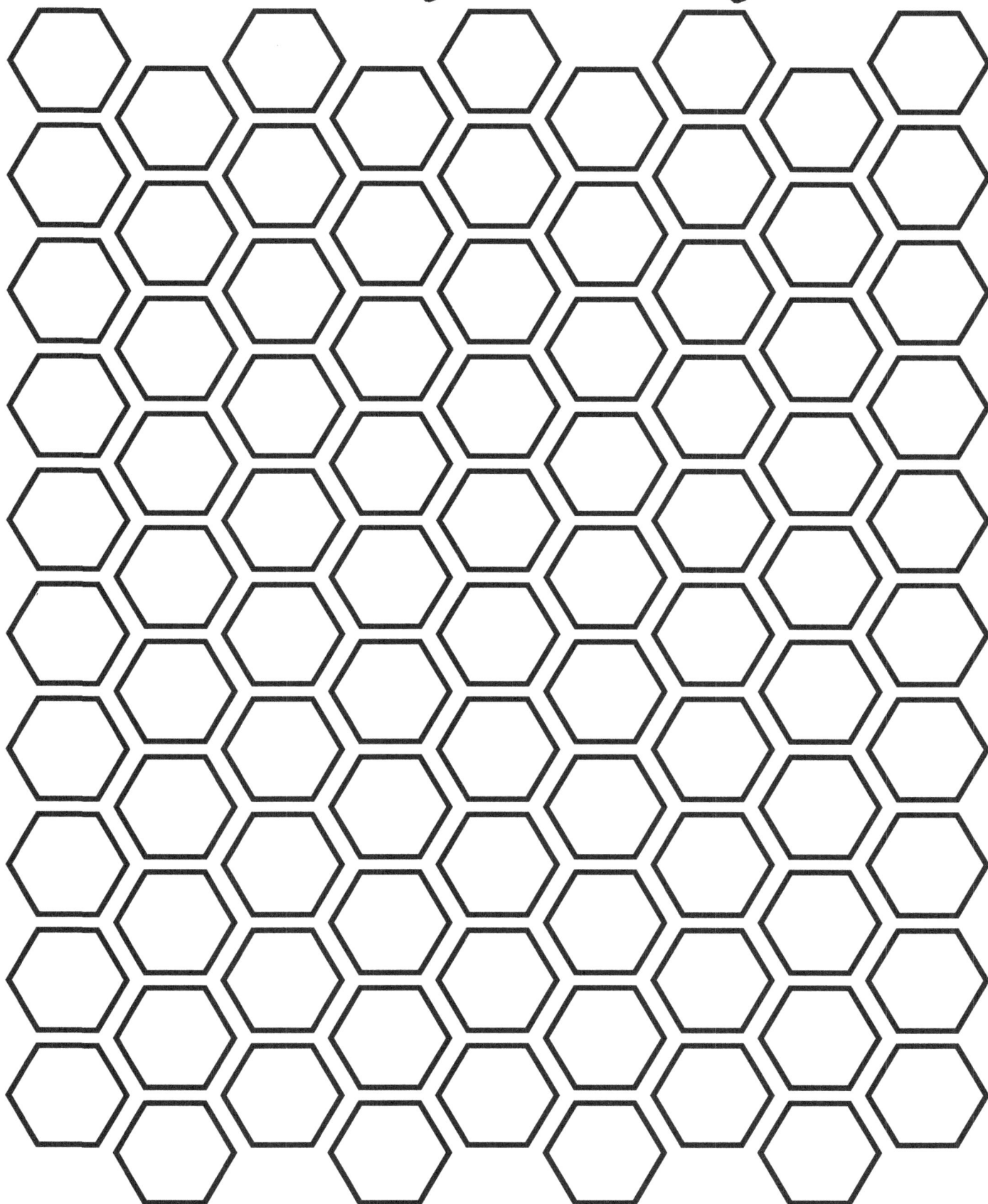

Colorful
Swearing Dreams

Swear Word Coloring Book for Adults

It takes a BIG HEART to TEACH LITTLE DIPSHITS

Colorful

Swearing Dreams

Swear Word Coloring Book for Adults

I CAN'T TEACH YOU TO BE SMART YOU ARE JUST A 12-YEAR-OLD DUMBASS

Colorful Swearing Dreams

Swear Word Coloring Book for Adults

I've tried to STOP SWEARING But I CUNT

Colorful
Swearing Dreams

Swear Word Coloring Book for Adults

I'm a 7TH GRADE TEACHER I'm not a FUCKING MAGICIAN

Colorful Swearing Dreams

Swear Word Coloring Book for Adults

KIDS are DICKS PARENTS are ASSHOLES This Day SUCKS BALLS

Colorful

Swearing Dreams

Swear Word Coloring Book for Adults

Parents Call them "ANGELS" Teachers Call them "SHITBALLS"

Colorful Swearing Dreams

Swear Word Coloring Book for Adults

5 MINUTES with these LITTLE BASTARDS and I'm Already EXHAUSTED AS FUCK

Colorful Swearing Dreams

Swear Word Coloring Book for Adults

Good Teachers CHANGE LIVES

Good Students SHUT the FUCK Up

Colorful Swearing Dreams

Swear Word Coloring Book for Adults

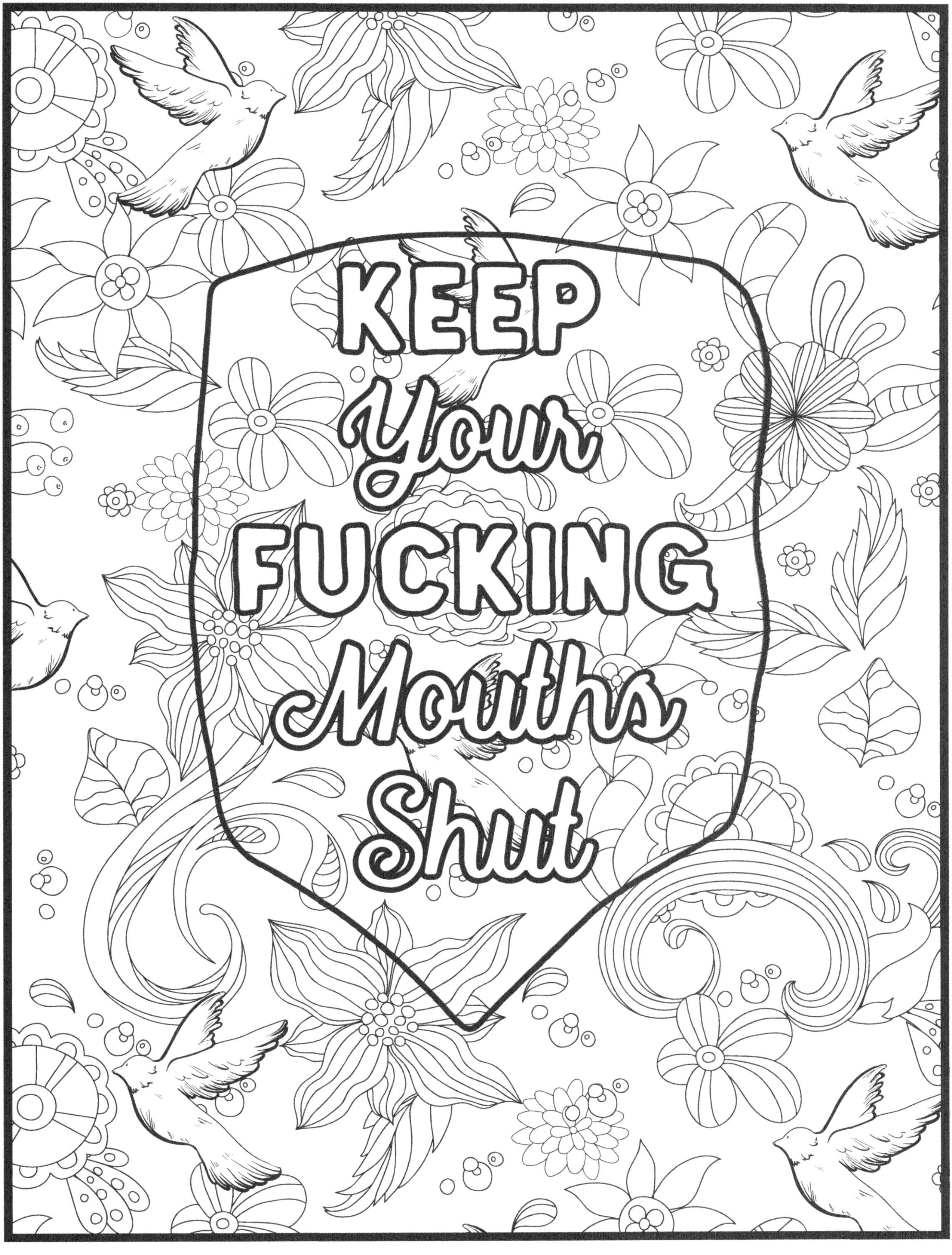
KEEP
Your
FUCKING
Mouths
Shut

Colorful

Swearing Dreams

Swear Word Coloring Book for Adults

PARENTS, Admitting Your Child is an ASSHOLE is the First Step

Colorful

Swearing Dreams

Swear Word Coloring Book for Adults

My
Week
is such a
CLUSTERFUCK
I'm a
7TH GRADE
TEACHER

Colorful Swearing Dreams

Swear Word Coloring Book for Adults

I Already TOLD YOU and you didn't FUCHING Listen

Colorful

Swearing Dreams

Swear Word Coloring Book for Adults

Teaching

Fucktards

is HARD

Colorful Swearing Dreams

Swear Word Coloring Book for Adults

Be a 7TH GRADE TEACHER They said It will be FUN They said You Gotta be SHITTING ME

Colorful Swearing Dreams

Swear Word Coloring Book for Adults

10 MINUTES in the CLASSROOM and I Feel like using "FUCK" AS A COMMA

Colorful Swearing Dreams

Swear Word Coloring Book for Adults

I'm FRESH Out of FUCKS to Give Today

Colorful

Swearing Dreams

Swear Word Coloring Book for Adults

STAFF MEETING AKA THE ART OF NOT GIVING A FUCK

Colorful Swearing Dreams

Swear Word Coloring Book for Adults

FUCK OFF
MONDAY

FUCK OFF
KIDS

Colorful

Swearing Dreams

Swear Word Coloring Book for Adults

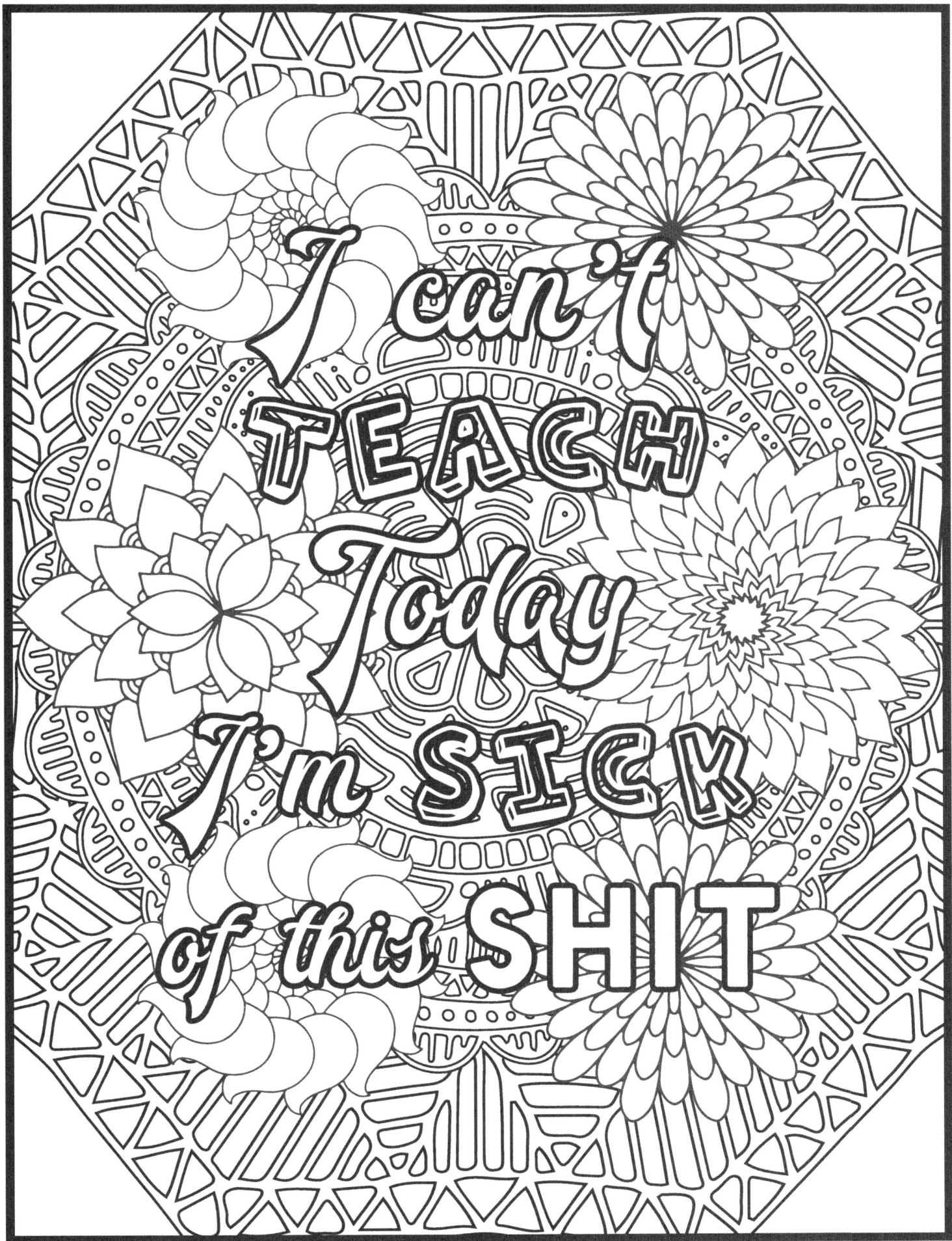

I can't TEACH Today I'm SICK of this SHIT

Colorful Swearing Dreams

Swear Word Coloring Book for Adults

I haven't Peed in 6 hours, I'm going to LOSE my SHIT in 3, 2, 1....

Colorful Swearing Dreams

Swear Word Coloring Book for Adults

Colorful Swearing Dreams

How is your stress level now?

Would you be kind enough to review our book?

Did the book allow you to put all the stress out of your mind, body and soul?
Hopefully you now feel fulfilled, relaxed and happy.

We sure put a lot of effort to provide you the best product possible that fits all your needs.

YOUR REVIEW is extremely valuable to us.
We don't see it as just a star rating, we read and study the feedbacks so we can
consistently improve our products to shape them how you want them to be.

We take pride in making quality products for your satisfaction.

That is why, we would really appreciate if you can take few minutes of your time and
leave us a review on our product's page.
That way, not only you will help other customers to make the right decision but
you will also allow us to make other quality products that can make funny & unique
gifts for your friends and family to just make them happy!

Colorful

Swearing Dreams

Swear Word Coloring Book for Adults

Made in the USA
Coppell, TX
09 March 2022